Njinga of Ndongo and Matamba

CHERRY LAKE PRESS

Published in the United States of America by Cherry Lake Publishing Group
Ann Arbor, Michigan
www.cherrylakepublishing.com

Reading Adviser: Beth Walker Gambro, MS, Ed., Reading Consultant, Yorkville, IL
Book Design: Jennifer Wahi
Illustrator: Jeff Bane

Photo Credits: University of Illinois Urbana-Champaign University Library, Public domain, via Wikimedia Commons, 5; *The Destruction of Black Civilization* by Chancellor Williams, Public domain via Internet Archive, 7 and 22; © Parinya Feungchan/Shutterstock, 9; © Njinga, Reine d'Angola. A Relação de AntonioCavazzi de Montecuccolo., CC BY-SA 4.0 via Wikimedia Commons, 11; Achille Devéria, Public domain, via Wikimedia Commons, 13 and 23; © Shutterstock.AI/Shutterstock, 15; Diego Velázquez, Public domain, via Wikimedia Commons, 17; © Shutterstock.AI/Shutterstock, 19; © Zute Lightfoot/Alamy Stock Photo, 21

Cherry Lake Press is an imprint of Cherry Lake Publishing Group

Library of Congress Cataloging-in-Publication Data

Names: Loh-Hagan, Virginia, author.
Title: Njinga of Ndongo and Matamba / written by: Virginia Loh-Hagan.
Description: Ann Arbor, Michigan : Cherry Lake Publishing, [2024] | Series: My itty-bitty bio | Audience: Grades K-1 | Summary: "Nzinga of Ndongo and Matamba was a strong African queen, ruling over the Ambundu Kingdoms of Ndongo and Matamba. This biography for early readers examines her life in a simple, age-appropriate way that helps young readers develop word recognition and reading skills. This title helps all readers learn about a historical female leader who made a difference in our world. The My Itty-Bitty Bio series celebrates diversity and inclusion, values that readers of all ages can aspire to" -- Provided by publisher.
Identifiers: LCCN 2023035027 | ISBN 9781668937761 (hardcover)
| ISBN 9781668938805 (paperback) | ISBN 9781668940143 (ebook)
| ISBN 9781668941492 (pdf)
Subjects: LCSH: Nzinga, Queen of Matamba, 1582-1663--Juvenile literature. | Queens--Angola--Biography--Juvenile literature.
Classification: LCC DT1365.N95 L64 2023 | DDC 967.3/01092
  [B]--dc23/eng/20230809
LC record available at https://lccn.loc.gov/2023035027

Printed in the United States of America

About the author: When not writing, Dr. Virginia Loh-Hagan serves as the Director of the Asian Pacific Islander Desi American (APIDA) Center at San Diego State University. She is also the Co-Executive Director of The Asian American Education Project. She lives in San Diego with her very tall husband and very naughty dogs.

About the illustrator: Jeff Bane and his two business partners own a studio along the American River in Folsom, California, home of the 1849 Gold Rush. When Jeff's not sketching or illustrating for clients, he's either swimming or kayaking in the river to relax.

I was born in 1583. My family ruled Angola. Angola is in Africa.

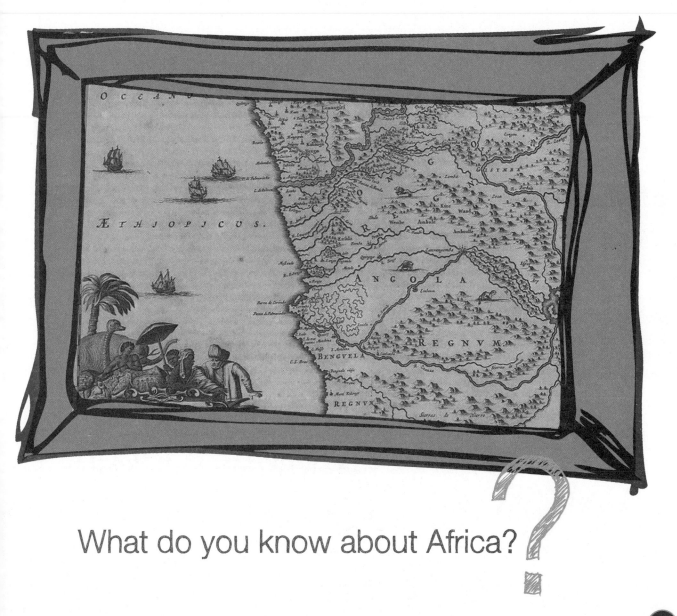

What do you know about Africa?

My father was king. He trained
me. I became a **warrior**. I fought
with him.

I was smart. I made war plans.
I loved using an axe.

What is your favorite tool?

I went to his meetings. I talked to people. I learned to make peace.

My father died. My brother became king. Then, he died. I became queen.

13

I was a girl. I wasn't meant to rule. Many were unhappy. They tried to take my power.

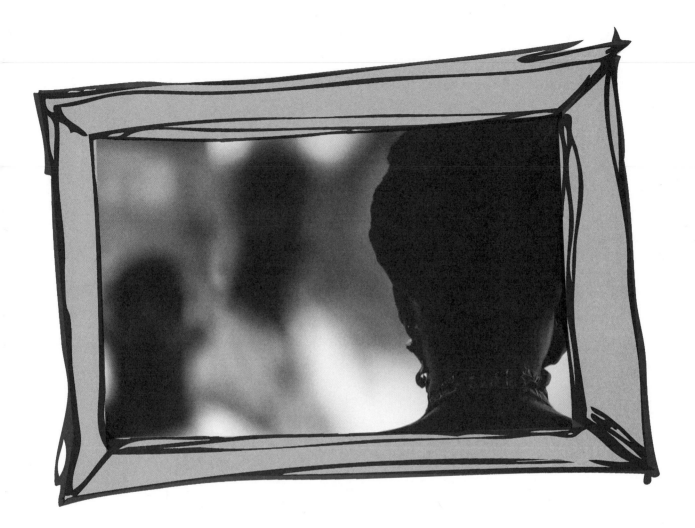

15

Many attacked. **Europeans** tried to **conquer** us. They tried to make us slaves.

I wanted peace. But I wasn't scared to fight. I fought in many wars. I fought for my people.

I died in 1663. But my **legacy** lives on. I was an African woman king.

What would you like to ask me?

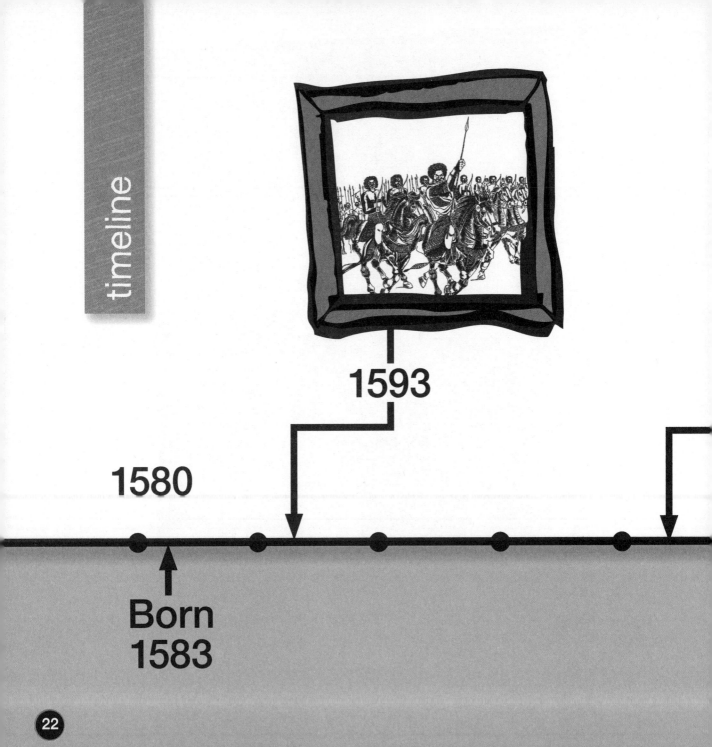

1593

1580

Born 1583

1624

1680

Died
1663

glossary

conquer (KAHN-ker) to attack in order to take control

Europeans (yer-uh-PEE-uhnz) people from Europe

legacy (LEH-guh-see) anything passed down from a person in the past

warrior (WOR-yer) a fighter

index